Montessori Toddler Discipline

7 Steps to Raising a Smart, Curious, and Responsible Child

Ralph Smith

© Copyright 2022 - All rights reserved.

The content contained within this book may not be reproduced, duplicated or transmitted without direct written permission from the author or the publisher.

Under no circumstances will any blame or legal responsibility be held against the publisher, or author, for any damages, reparation, or monetary loss due to the information contained within this book, either directly or indirectly.

Legal Notice:

This book is copyright protected. It is only for personal use. You cannot amend, distribute, sell, use, quote or paraphrase any part, or the content within this book, without the consent of the author or publisher.

Disclaimer Notice:

Please note the information contained within this document is for educational and entertainment purposes only. All effort has been executed to present accurate, up to date, reliable, complete information. No warranties of any kind are declared or implied. Readers acknowledge that the author is not engaged in the rendering of legal, financial, medical or professional advice. The content within this book has been derived from various sources. Please consult a licensed professional before attempting any techniques outlined in this book.

By reading this document, the reader agrees that under no circumstances is the author responsible for any losses, direct or indirect, that are incurred as a result of the use of the information contained within this document, including, but not limited to, errors, omissions, or inaccuracies.

Table of Contents

INTRODUCTION 1

CHAPTER 1: ENVIRONMENT 5
    MONTESSORI-TRAINED ADULTS 6
    ORGANIZED, STIMULATING, BUT NOT CLUTTERED 10
    EMOTIONAL ENVIRONMENT 11
    PROPER TOOLS FOR THIS METHOD 14

CHAPTER 2: COMMUNICATION 17
    RELATIONSHIPS WORK BOTH WAYS 19
    BOTH PARTIES ARE ALLOWED TO VOICE THEIR EMOTIONS 20
    HONESTY AIDS IN OTHER STEPS 22

CHAPTER 3: RESPONSIBILITY 25
    HOW TO HELP OTHERS 26
    HOW ACTIONS LEAD TO CONSEQUENCES 27
    HOW THEY ARE RESPONSIBLE FOR THEMSELVES AND HOW THEY TREAT OTHERS 29
    TEACHING THEM TO DECIDE THINGS FOR THEMSELVES 30

CHAPTER 4: FREEDOM 33
    ALLOWING CHILDREN TO THINK AND FEEL FOR THEMSELVES 34
    STILL SUPPORTING YOUR CHILD TO DECIDE THINGS THEMSELVES 36
    EMPOWERING YOUR CHILD'S CHOICES 37
    APPLAUDING BOTH WINS AND LOSSES 38

CHAPTER 5: EMPOWERMENT 41
    ENCOURAGING INTRINSIC MOTIVATION 47
    STILL SUPPORTING YOUR CHILD TO DECIDE THINGS THEMSELVES 48
    EMPOWERING YOUR CHILD'S CHOICES 50
    APPLAUDING BOTH WINS AND LOSSES 54

CHAPTER 6: MISBEHAVIOR 57

Prioritizing Misbehaviors 58
Deciding What Behaviors Are Accidental or Natural and What Is Learned Behavior 59
Not Enforcing Harsh Punishments 61

CHAPTER 7: LIFE, SIMULATED... 65

Ensuring Your Child Is Ready for Real Life 67
Ensuring These Lessons Will Mean They Can Think for Themselves 68
Allowing Them to Be Able to Be Free in Life to Do Things 70

CONCLUSION... 73

REFERENCES 79

Introduction

The foundation of Montessori education is to naturally develop your student or child rather than give them a traditional education in which the teacher hands the information to the student without giving them opportunities to practice or the means to use it in life. When applying this to toddler discipline, it means we discipline the child with a guiding hand, using tools that will enable them to eventually make their own well-informed decisions in life from a younger age than compared with conventional disciplining. Here are some strategies to help you implement Montessori discipline:

- Use clear language.

- Emphasize cause and effect using "if-then phrasing"

- Use a variety of natural consequences.

- Validate emotions.

- Avoid brides, rewards, and punishments.

- Keep communication respectful.

- Model how to make amends.

- Find ways to solve problems together.

- Give room for freedom within kind and clear limits.

- Translate for your child.

From the Montessori perspective, the definition of the toddler age begins when the child begins to walk (or toddle) around their environment in order to explore the fascinating (and sometimes a little dangerous) world around them. This is generally around one year old, although some children begin walking as early as nine months. The child has suddenly realized they have more autonomy over their movement and choices. They no longer need a parent to carry them to that interesting-looking box across the room. They want to walk, run, climb, and explore using their own unsteady yet rapidly developing abilities. The toddler stage ends around three years old when the child becomes more steady on their feet and has learned the skills needed to begin to keep up with older children.

According to the Montessori discipline, some of the developmental needs of toddlers include:

- gross motor skills like walking, running, and jumping

- fine motor skills like feeding themselves, buttoning, zipping, and drawing; this helps with their sense of touch by allowing the child to become aware of how to do things themselves within their surroundings

- sensory recognition of colors, scents, and things that are hot/cold, soft/hard, smooth/bumpy, etc; this increases the toddler's development of their senses and helps them to recognize what is useful and what is not

- language skill-building of robust single words or short simple sentences to enable them to communicate their needs. Toddlers need to learn how to communicate what they feel because parents are not always able to understand what it is they want when they throw a fit. It also teaches proper behavior in social environments.

- social skill-building to allow them to engage in parallel play, play with others, and take turns. This teaches respect and empathy for their peers as they learn that they cannot just grab things or bully others. Sharing and understanding that a toy is being used helps them develop these skills.

The Montessori toddler environment allows the child to explore outcomes with curiosity and experience both success and failure safely. This allows them to feel confident in their growing skills as they reach the end of their toddler years and are ready for the next developmental stage. Creating a stimulating but safe space for a toddler to feel free to explore, make a mess, express their feelings, and take responsibility for their own choices takes some thought and planning. That work is well worth it when you begin to watch your toddler grow in confidence and ability within the space you've carefully designed just for them and their educational, social-emotional, and physical development.

Chapter 1:

Environment

Fostering an environment that enables your child to develop confident and competent independence is the foundation for a good Montessori education. There are four elements to help create that foundational environment for toddlers:

- Adults who are familiar with the Montessori approach and who will avoid "baby talk" and use appropriate words that help build a child's vocabulary and understanding of themselves, their peers, and the world.

- Designated and well-defined space for free exploration of learning materials that foster curiosity and creativity, a space for activities that build gross motor development, a quiet area with sleeping mats, and a food area that allows a child to help prepare, serve, eat, and clean up snacks and meals.

- Child-sized tables, chairs, step-stools, cooking, and cleaning tools to allow children to learn to handle diverse tasks independently.

- An atmosphere of calm respect and control modeled by the patient, soft-spoken adults and fostered by compassionate support when the child needs behavioral guidance.

Montessori-Trained Adults

Safety, comfort, and respect can be provided, demonstrated, and reinforced throughout the day with the support of adults well-trained in the Montessori method. In addition, confusing messages are avoided when all the adults are approaching communication and discipline with the same process.

The hallmarks of Montessori training require the adult to do these things:

- **Avoid baby talk.** Using the correct words helps build the child's vocabulary and communicates respect for the child and the communication process. It also encourages them to take responsibility for understanding how to communicate their needs while also understanding the needs of others.

- **Reinforce natural consequences stemming from your toddler's action.** It is important that a Montessori-trained adult never use bribes, rewards, or punishments to influence a child's behavior. Instead, the natural consequences of the child's own actions and decisions can be gently explained. Alternative actions can be explored with the child through reading a book or discussing other action options after the child has calmed down and is open to learning a new way to manage their feelings. For example, if a child becomes overwhelmed or frustrated when they lose a game and overturn the game board, throw pieces, or otherwise express their feelings in a negative way, the adult may step in and help the child learn to recognize and change unacceptable behavior. The adult can respect the toddler's feelings while firmly but quietly redirecting them to an activity that will help them lower their sense of overwhelm or frustration so that the adult can then discuss other ways the child can handle losing a game in the future. This is an age when children want to be more proficient than their new skills allow them to be, and learning how to regulate big emotions is an important component of the Montessori approach.

- **Treat the child respectfully.** Avoid yelling, shaming, and blaming. Be gentle but firm in discussing the child's choices as well as the limits and boundaries within the environment. A Montessori approach begins with knowing the child. This means observing the child and understanding their personality and the level of skill that can be expected in a certain activity, as well as the particular skills the child is actively working to develop. For example, when a toddler begins to learn to climb, falls are to be expected, even in a well-thought-out safe space. Some toddlers fall, blink, pick themselves up, and try again. Others get more quickly frustrated and will therefore benefit from adult modeling of how to handle disappointment, falling down, skinned knees, or bumps and bruises. Still others will push the limits of the environmental boundaries, climbing things not meant to be climbed or climbing in a dangerous manner. These children will need more hands-on redirection in which the adult identifies safe yet challenging activities that will satisfy the child's need for exploration while still allowing them to learn how to respect the rules of their safe space.

- **Encourage autonomy within appropriate boundaries**. Adults do not do *for* the child in a Montessori educational approach, they do *with* the child by reinforcing the child's own recognized capabilities verbally and allowing a child to stretch and grow those capabilities as appropriate. This could involve patiently explaining that one toy must be cleaned up before another is chosen, walking a child through the steps to find a solution to a problem, or translating one child's feelings and actions to another so that respectful communication can occur between children. For the very young toddler, some physical intervention may be necessary while they are learning what they are expected to do. For example, a child who has just learned to walk and is unsteady on their feet may need to hold an adult's hand when carrying a toy back to the shelf or may need the adult to help carry the toy under the child's direction. Once the child can carry the toy themself, adult intervention stops. If the child is confused or asks for adult intervention when they no longer need it, the adult then communicates to the child, in a positive manner, that they have learned a new skill and no longer need help.

The good news for adults who use the Montessori approach is that toddlers who are given structured autonomy over their own environment and choices are less prone to unexplained meltdowns and tantrums. Instead, their frustration, anger, or inhibition will be clearly linked to a skill they are trying to build (losing a game, falling off a slide, breaking a crayon, wanting a toy that another child is currently playing with, spilling their drink, etc.). This makes it easier for the adult to redirect the child in a way that calms them while also giving the child the proper language to explore what they are feeling and why they are feeling that way.

Organized, Stimulating, but Not Cluttered

A stimulating but clutter-free organized environment is a hallmark of a Montessori approach to developing a child who can make choices and decisions for themselves and who can accept responsibility for their choices and their environment while respecting others in the same space. As many activities as a child can manage on their own or with minimal adult supervision should be accessible in a neat and orderly arrangement.

At the toddler age, it is expected that the younger toddlers will need more adult supervision and prompting, but at all times the environment should be set up to allow even the youngest child to figure out as much as possible on their own. For example, a toddler space should contain the following items:

- Colorful soft cushions and rugs that the child can carry on their own to whatever activity is required, and then put back in their proper place when it is no longer needed.

- Age-appropriate educational books and activities placed in labeled bins or on low shelves so that the child can access them on their own as well as put them away on their own, helping to keep the environment clutter-free.

- Toddler-appropriate cleaning supplies like rags and small spray bottles with non-toxic cleaning liquid so that children can clean up their own areas after playing or making a spill.

- Spaces with defined purposes, such as a reading corner with scattered cushions and rugs next to the bookshelves, or an eating area with easy-to-reach snack items, small tables and chairs, and child-sized pouring containers and scoops to enable a child to fix their own snacks.

In an ordered environment the toddler learns—by direct instruction of adults and by watching slightly older toddlers—how to choose an activity while also keeping the environment uncluttered and clean. Obviously, at the toddler stage, adults are needed to remind and guide children to take the necessary steps until these have become solid self-directed habits. The more a toddler can do by themselves, the more quickly they will develop confidence and competence.

Emotional Environment

They don't call the toddler age the "Terrible Twos" for no reason. Toddlers have newfound mobility but are faced with many barriers to exercising this mobility that cause frustration. Falling, not being able to reach things that are up high, not being strong enough to carry things without losing their balance, and more are all challenges a toddler faces every day. When it comes to language, they are learning 2–3 new words a day, both the meaning of the word and how to use it to get what they want or explain how they feel. The Montessori approach gives the toddler control which, in turn, gives them a sense of emotional safety. That sense of emotional safety comes from knowing the routine will be followed, the space is well-defined, the toys and books and learning opportunities are age-appropriate, and the adults are there to guide and help with empathy and respect.

The Montessori environment is structured to allow children to learn to control their emotions without shame and blame. There is no need for loud voices or harsh punishment. Instead, consistent routines and rules, gentle but firm reminders, and clear communication in a well-structured environment serve to model for the child how to behave. A dedicated quiet space for an overwhelmed child to retreat and gain control of their own frustration allows the child to learn to self-regulate and understand appropriate and respectful social interaction.

Adults in the Montessori environment communicate boundaries and expected social skills, such as saying thank you and you're welcome, with quiet reminders and prompts. When a child becomes upset or frustrated, changing to another activity can often reset the emotional reaction. This does not mean that the behavior or out-of-bounds action is not addressed. Instead, it means that the child is offered the opportunity to calm down so that they can better understand the negative consequences of their behavior and help brainstorm other actions they can take the next time they are upset or frustrated. Adult instruction in brainstorming natural consequences and alternative behaviors for toddlers often includes books or modeling that introduce the concept to the child in a non-threatening way.

Empathy is a hallmark of respectful communication, and the child is not punished for being angry or frustrated but offered the opportunity to change their environment or activity to one that will not make them angry or frustrated. A toddler may also be given time to calm themselves in an appropriate space with an activity that does not require talking or communicating such as a puzzle or some other activity they can do independently. Respectful communication is best when it is done in a calm, non-confrontational manner, especially with a toddler who is learning the language and how to handle their emotions through communication rather than by the non-verbal means they used as infants.

Emotions are always recognized and respected in a Montessori environment, so an angry child is not asked to stop showing anger or other strong emotion but is instead directed to change their activity or ask for help with any task that may be causing the emotion. Adults feeling a strong emotion may also label that emotion, as long as the adult does not shame or blame the child for their emotion. Instead of, "You make me angry," say, "I get angry when someone hits me." Communicating clearly that strong emotion is a natural response to some situations and is also experienced by adults (who are modeling control of their emotions) allows the toddler to understand there is a path to identifying, labeling, and managing their own emotions.

If the anger is expressed physically by one child to another or is caused when two children don't agree on rules or cannot share, then adults step in to model respectful communication and help both children find the right solution for their disagreement. For toddlers, this may include talking through a set of rules they can both agree on or having the children separate and do calming activities on their own.

Learning to self-calm and respectfully work through disagreements is a foundational skill for lifelong success, so another tool to help children develop these skills is reading books with them or using cards with words and pictures that talk about how to understand and deal with strong emotions like anger, fear, sadness, and frustration.

Proper Tools for This Method

The Montessori environment is rich with opportunities for children to try their own hand at developing their skills. Books, toys that help develop fine motor skills such as busy boards that offer many kinds of zippers, snaps, buttons, and laces to open and close, as well as games that promote gross motor skills should be easily available for the child to choose for play.

When creating a safe and secure environment for toddlers, make sure the toys are chosen with the age of the user in mind, and avoid toys with small pieces a young child may swallow or choke on.

Toddlers love to explore while developing their motor skills, so having some short ladders, stairsteps, or safe climbing areas in the play space can help them build these skills without the risk of injuring themselves. Outdoor areas can have swings, slides, scooters, bikes, and trikes.

Eating areas should have snacks and meals easily accessible to the child. The tables and chairs should be child-sized so that there is no need for a booster seat or high chair for toddlers. Unbreakable containers, scoops, and utensils offer the child an opportunity to build fine motor skills like pouring and serving.

Everything, of course, should be appropriately child-sized so that the child can do most of the activities without much, if any, adult help.

Chapter 2:

Communication

Ensuring open and honest communication between adult and child requires creating clear guidelines. Toddlers know what they feel, but they often don't have the words to express those feelings. During infancy they had only a few ways to express themselves: laughter, crying, reaching out, or pulling back. By the age of three, a toddler generally has learned and begun to use 900–1,000 new words, according to the Mayo clinic. At two, Mayo asserts they typically may only have 50 words they use regularly. That's a lot of new words for a developing toddler to learn to use effectively in the span of just one year, and Montessori principles help them do so in a self-empowering way.

Given the fact that younger toddlers may not have many words to express all the emotions, wishes, desires, and fears they are having, adults need to be exceptionally tuned in to the child and their personality and abilities. In addition, they need to be clear and concise when helping a younger toddler understand what is going on in their own bodies and minds when they are feeling strong emotions. The Montessori approach encourages giving children the appropriate words they need to express how they feel and ask for what they want without baby talk and in a direct and concise way. You have opened a communication path if a toddler nods when you ask, "Do you feel angry?" This can be followed up with a quick moment of empathy, "I feel angry when I spill my drink, too."

Once the toddler has a name for the emotion, they may be ready to choose a calming action, such as cleaning up the spill, changing activities, or asking for any necessary adult help. At this point, the adult can offer a few directed choices for the child to make about what comes next. "I feel better after I clean up my spill. Would you like to do that now?" The communication follows the child's cues and focuses on empathy and clarity. One child might immediately jump up to get the cleaning supplies, while another may still be embroiled in the emotion and begin to cry. In that case, the adult may offer another direct choice, "Would you like my help cleaning up the spill?" If the child nods, then the adult can help redirect the child by giving them a small task such as, "Would you get the spray bottle for me?" If the child is not even capable of getting the spray bottle because they are so mired in the emotion, the adult can continue expressing empathy, get the spray bottle, and ask the child to spray and wipe up the spill. Modeling the steps of the behavior being encouraged while providing the specific language is extremely important for toddlers who are learning so much and building so many skills every day.

Adults need to offer toddlers proactive guidance, directed choices, and a chance to slow down and process their emotions when necessary. For children who are at the beginning of learning to use language, adults may use touch and non-verbal cues when asking the child to stop or become quiet.

Relationships Work Both Ways

Perhaps the most important lesson for the toddler developmental stage is that other people have feelings and deserve respect, too. This is a dawning concept for children in the toddler stage. Infants don't fully comprehend that when they bite, it hurts the person they are biting. As they move into the toddler stage, they begin to learn that the things that cause them pain (or fear, or joy, or pleasure) also cause others to feel the same thing. They also learn that some of their actions can cause others to change their actions. For example, if a child is playing with a toy the toddler wants to play with, a well-timed bite can chase off the other child and free up the toy for the biter. Obviously, that is not a behavior that fosters an atmosphere of respect and proper boundaries.

What the complex reality of mutual respect means for their actions and behaviors can be confusing to a toddler who just wants what they want. Adults can model this by voicing the rules, as well as their own emotions and requests, in a calm and respectful manner at the same time they are helping the child find the words to voice their desire for a toy another child is playing with. Modeling how the toddler may ask for a turn to play with the toy is a foundational Montessori skill. For toddlers, this can be frustrating because, in the Montessori environment, a child is free to say no to sharing a toy.

Because toddlers have trouble giving voice to their own feelings, adults should expand the toddler's growing awareness of their own and others' feelings by reading age-appropriate books on those topics with them. Books help toddlers to learn behaviors that are respectful to others, like asking for a turn, by giving them the language to express their own feelings in a relatable manner. When the concept is initially difficult for the toddler to absorb, an adult may voice those feelings for the toddler if necessary.

Both Parties Are Allowed to Voice Their Emotions

Part of the Montessori approach is to encourage sharing but not create arbitrary sharing mandates such as time limits for playing with a toy or requiring that all children do the same activity at the same time under the teacher's direction. For toddlers, this can be confusing. When the toddler wants to play with a toy, their desire is high and their empathy for the child who is currently playing with the toy is low. Creating simple rules that encourage autonomy, respect, and communication can help a toddler develop confidence, empathy, and patience.

These rules are fairly simple, but can be difficult for toddlers to manage without adult guidance at first:

- Each child gets a turn to express themself without interruption.

- No judgment ("you were wrong" or "you did something bad"), just honest communication ("I get angry when my toy is yanked out of my hands" or "my arm hurts when you hit it").

- Child-led solutions even if the adult thinks they don't sound fair; the children will prefer to come up with their own mutually agreed-upon solutions.

- Safety is always first; if physical or emotional safety is threatened, children are separated until they are calm and ready to discuss.

- A calm discussion is a productive discussion; allow time for the children to calm down if necessary.

- Never force an apology.

Following a few simple rules of respectful communication helps even a toddler whose lexicon is limited express themselves and feel heard and respected. With toddlers, use the language and concepts they are familiar with already or facilitate the discussion by reading and discussing an appropriate book about sharing, or listening, or not fighting.

Honesty Aids in Other Steps

Forcing an apology is never acceptable in the Montessori method. Forced apologies feel like lies to the child who is told to offer an apology they don't mean and sound insincere to the child who receives the apology. Worse, forcing an apology often closes off the communication path and prevents the toddlers from learning to feel empathy and respect for others. This leads the child to become unappreciative of their peers and they may lose trust in their relationships. Children are highly susceptible to energies, and they can tell when someone is lying to them. Teach your child to apologize when and if they hurt someone, but also teach them to be sincere with it.

Instead, modeling and guiding toddlers on how to respectfully express their honest feelings can help them understand what they are feeling, why they are feeling it, and how to express their feelings instead of passing judgment against another person. For example, guiding a child to recognize the difference between "I don't want you to bite me" (an honest "I" statement) and "I hate you" (a transitory emotional judgment that doesn't get down to the root of the problem) helps them to solve the problem faster because they become aware of what they feel in that moment. If they do not want to get bitten, then they will try to find a solution that makes everyone happy and diffuses the tempers. However, if they ignore that instinct then they will lash out with their emotional feelings and create even more problems as their emotions tend to be overwhelming and therefore overexaggerated in the moment.

For toddlers, like for people of all ages, knowing the root of the problem helps them get to a solution much faster. If they are able to understand and create a coherent path toward the solution, they are more likely to use that as a means to keep themselves safe. This is what we call motivation and empowerment (a subject to be discussed in later chapters). Another characteristic that is the result of children using honesty as a way to aid themselves and others is responsibility. If the child is able to take responsibility for their actions, reactions, and responses to situations, then they are listening to that inner voice—their instinct—and using what is beneficial for them to guide their way instead of letting peers and the outside world control them.

Chapter 3:

Responsibility

Teaching children responsibility and consequences is one of the main goals of parents and teachers. The Montessori method incorporates those two concepts into every aspect of the toddler's day by giving the child as much freedom within a safe environment as possible; however, with freedom comes consequences. By dealing with the consequences of their own freely-chosen actions, the toddler develops confidence and competence in making the many small decisions that crop up during the day: what to have for a snack, when to nap, when to wake up, what to play with, how to overcome disappointment, how to handle the unexpected, or even how to handle transitions from one activity to another.

What this does for the toddler is it engages their developing brain and creates a question-and-answer scenario for the child. When the child asks a question, there are multiple outcomes to the scenario; the toddler then needs to freely decide what the best outcome is for themself as well as others.

The Montessori method helps the toddler learn these life lessons by providing the necessary tools used to approach life situations. In order for the child to learn, they first have to make a mistake. As a parent, you may tend to want to immediately protect your child, find ways to make sure they apologize for their error, or teach them a lesson. This is something that should be avoided as it can cause the toddler to feel angry, stressed, or scared. Instead, gently wait to see how they react, create encouraging steps that will lead them to an outcome of growth and learning, then help them feel better.

How to Help Others

Toddlers are emerging from infancy where they are completely dependent upon others to feed, bathe, and move them. They may have a rudimentary understanding that biting their mother while nursing will result in their mother reacting sharply. In the toddler development stage, however, they will begin to understand that when you bite another child, they will bite back, or hit, or cry loudly. This will lead them to recognize that their actions can have unwanted consequences. Their growing language skills will allow them to recognize that they can use words instead of physical actions to indicate their own feelings and concerns, as well as enable them to start listening to the feelings and concerns of others around them.

This is the perfect time for toddlers to learn how they can use their newfound mobility to help others. The Montessori environment encourages children to demonstrate a skill they've learned to another child who is still in the learning stage of the same skill, to encourage the other child verbally without doing the task for them, and to celebrate when another child masters the new skill.

For example, at snack time, a toddler who has learned how to scoop out their snack without making a spill may at first be inclined to do the task for another toddler who has not learned how. With adult guidance, however, the toddler learns to ask if the other child would like help and then offers suggestions (don't fill the scoop so full, put the bowl closer to the container, etc.). In this way, both of the toddlers are learning—one how to fix a snack without making a mess and the other how to help someone without taking over and doing the task for them.

How Actions Lead to Consequences

The freedom to choose means accepting the consequences of the choice. This is often hard for adults, so it is no surprise that toddlers need adult guidance in building this skill. If you pour your own snack, you may spill it. If you spill it, you must then clean it up. In the Montessori environment, spills are not judged as good or bad. They are spills, and the natural consequence of a spill is to clean up. Because a Montessori environment is equipped with cleaning supplies accessible to the toddler, this is easy for them to do without having to call for adult help (and possibly adult judgment). That removal of judgment helps assert the child within their environment and makes them feel safe. This allows the child to see how every action has a reaction, whether it is "good" or "bad." However, try to steer clear of using the terms "good" and "bad" as they can be used as rewards or punishments for the toddler. Opening the child up to the fact that there are consequences also helps them see that there are rewards, too. This creates a balance within their life, an equal scale of what is socially acceptable and what is not.

There are more social consequences to be learned, too. If a toddler doesn't share, then other toddlers are less likely to share with them. The Montessori approach of guiding children to communicate and exploring these issues by reading books that discuss sharing, or respecting others, or consequences of many sorts, will lead the child to learn to accept consequences as a natural part of learning. This gives them the confidence to find their own solutions as they continue to rapidly learn new skills and grow their vocabulary to communicate with others. The Montessori method has woven these beliefs within their practices because they want to help the child and the parents. Creating examples of how they should treat others the way they would like to be treated (the golden rule we have all heard) projects an image of the other toddlers' reactions towards them. If they do not wish to be ignored or left out, then they should not ignore or leave out others.

How They Are Responsible for Themselves and How They Treat Others

Responsibility is the natural outcome when a toddler learns to accept that they can find solutions for any of the consequences of their actions and decisions that have unexpected or undesired outcomes. For instance, if the toddler pushes another over, then they need to take responsibility for this action. In this case, the toddler might say they are sorry to the other toddler or help them back up. Taking responsibility leads the toddler to see positive reinforcement toward their actions In this same example, if they accidentally hurt someone, or see a fellow toddler hurting, offering them help positively reinforces their relationship. The toddler is not responsible for how the other toddler reacts or what they do, but simply for their own actions toward their peers. If they are able to see that their actions have positive outcomes, they are more likely to continue the pattern of good behavior because not only is it the right thing to do, but they get more internal satisfaction from it. That is what a toddler needs. That self-confidence and assurance that what they are doing is right.

Teaching responsibility for actions is just one of the skills that toddlers acquire as they age. They also learn that they need to be responsible for how they treat others, what they can bring to relationships—both with family members and friends—and how having empathetic awareness of others is the proper thing to do. For example, if they invite a friend over to their house, and that friend wants to play with all their toys, but the toddler feels protective of them, they must learn to relinquish control and set a limit. They cannot take the toy away from their friend. Their options are to simply ask for it instead or use another one. Understanding these relationships is helpful to a toddler, and though it is complex, the basics are: do to others what they would like done to themself. Toddlers learn by trial-and-error, so engaging with other toddlers and learning how to navigate emotional situations helps the toddler to see that being responsible benefits more people than just themself.

Teaching Them to Decide Things for Themselves

As a toddler grows, they become more curious. They begin seeking approval from their parents and peers, as well as finding new methods of learning—whether it be through sight, sense, touch, or taste—to ensure that they are heading in the right direction. While being validated from external forces is considered a "no-no" within the Montessori approach, toddlers have yet to learn the ability to separate external from internal. As a toddler's intellect begins to peek, they begin to try new things such as playing, speaking, counting, and other engaging activities that push their brain's development. However, as a parent, particularly a new parent, you might tend to over-help your toddler by trying to do things for them so that they do not throw a fit or get frustrated. What that does is actually harms the child's cerebral growth as they become dependent on their parents to do everything for them. Instead, try to find an environment that suits your child best and encourage them to decide for themselves what it is they need.

As the child ages, you will have to find the boundary between helping and allowing them the freedom to do things themselves. If the toddler wants to open something but is having difficulty, encourage them to keep trying until they get it open. Do not open it for them unless they have attempted it themself. Teaching your toddler to have their own freedom to learn things encourages mental growth, independence, and the ability to have patience. Being a source of positive support for your child is the best form of help they can get. While it is instinct to step in and do everything for your toddler, you must remember that they are not helpless. They are capable of doing things to a certain extent. Doing it for them only teaches them that they do not have to try very hard and that others will eventually do it for them. Please try to avoid that at all costs as it will lead to difficulties later in life and create habits that may not be so easy to break as an adult.

We learn as we grow. That is the biggest lesson everyone is taught from a very young age. In order to grow, we need to know that it is okay to fail. However, failure sometimes stems from negative feelings because of shame placed upon a person when they were a child. If your toddler makes an error, do not shame them for it. Instead, show them that making a mistake is good and that they will learn from that error. If they have not harmed anyone, there is no point in shaming the child. You can explain why it is not okay to constantly make the same mistake, but do not shame the toddler. That does not teach them freedom; instead, later in life, it creates resentment and the feeling of never being free. This is something the Montessori discipline method is trying to help parents avoid because it causes the child to shut down. Instead of making them feel bad, find ways to encourage them to do it by themself. This will stimulate the toddler and engage them in ways that are required when they are young. Many two-year-olds need constant stimulation; they are always touching or playing with something because they are naturally curious and are trying to understand what it is. This behavior should be encouraged to a certain extent. Make sure they are not hurting anyone during this period of growth.

Chapter 4:

Freedom

Setting clear boundaries but allowing them to do things freely is the healthy way of teaching your child. If they feel that there are too many rules, too many boundaries, then your toddler will be more likely to retaliate or rebel; however, if they have free reign to do as they please, they may grow up without regard for anyone else's safety, feelings, or opinions. Freedom is wonderful for toddlerhood, but only to a certain degree. Freedom within reason is the way to look at it. Allow your child to make decisions for themself but set clear boundaries on subjects, behaviors, and etiquette in order to keep their environment safe and chaos-free. Freedom is necessary for the toddler, as it is for anyone of any age, because it gives the person a sense of belonging, awareness, and respect for the opportunities granted to them; without that freedom, they can become reserved or feel hurt, which is something no parent wants for their child. This can be avoided if there is a level of respect, communication, and empowerment happening between the child and the parent.

Another form of freedom that was studied by Maria Montessori—the founder of the Montessori method—was called the Prepared Environment. What this entails is the adult studies the child, the way they act, speak, learn, etc., and creates an environment around that, an environment where the child can choose what sorts of activities to engage in, lessons to learn, and things to do based on their emotional attitude that day. For example, if a child uses the visual side of their brain, there should be activities left out for the child to do such as coloring, shapes to manipulate, and puzzles. If a toddler is more creative, there should be ways to draw or paint. If they are mathematically inclined, leave some counting or sorting activities. If the toddler has developmental issues or is handicapped in some way, create a prepared environment that suits their needs. This helps the child feel as though they have total freedom over their choices while the adult has created an environment that is beneficial for the toddler. The prepared environment is a useful tool to learn when teaching freedom to your toddler as it allows them to have the necessary techniques and devices at a certain time without overwhelming them or causing the toddler too much emotional stress. Removing stress, anxiety, and frustration creates more positive opportunities for the toddler, and they feel far more in control of not just their environment, but their emotions too. This creates stronger, healthier relational bonds.

Allowing Children to Think and Feel for Themselves

Freedom comes in many forms. Freedom can be the right to express oneself, to have valid emotional feelings toward a certain scenario, or even facilitate personal growth. Giving your child the freedom to think and feel for themself is teaching them self-discipline. This is a key part of growth as children need structure within their lives but also the freedom to explore what it is they need to understand the world. Giving the toddler the option to think for themself encourages them to deal with life stresses in a healthy way. It also demonstrates that they have the capability to understand what they are feeling without being confused. That is why most children throw tantrums—they are scared or confused. With the proper environmental tools, however, your toddler will learn to understand their needs better.

Giving the child the space to understand their emotions also increases their academic abilities, improves their health, and helps them to cope more easily. Freedom in the form of self-discipline teaches children at a young age to listen to their instincts and moral compass instead of being influenced by the outside world. This can stop many negative situations that children are faced with as they grow such as bullying, teasing, stealing, and more. Remember not to over-discipline your toddler as they will feel trapped and may be more likely to lash out. Instead, find the right balance of freedom and discipline.

Still Supporting Your Child to Decide Things Themselves

Every child needs support. Supporting the child in their life decisions while also guiding them toward the best possible outcome is what being a parent is all about. However, where things tend to get complicated and the lines begin to blur is when parents feel the need to ensure that their child grows up to be a productive and contributing member of their community and so they remove some of the toddler's freedom, sometimes subconsciously or inadvertently. Support is fantastic, but too much control from the parent's end causes resentment within the child. Understanding the boundary between positive support and controlling support is key to your toddler's success.

Positive support is when the child understands that they have the liberty to decide things for themselves, without the worry of mom or dad being terribly upset with them should their choice disagree with their parents' view. Giving the child your undivided attention when they speak helps the toddler feel that they are seen and respected. A gentle yet firm tone goes a long way. Try not to push your toddler—if they are not ready, that is okay. They will be ready on their own time.

Controlling support happens when a parent is supportive of their child's dreams, ideas, and wants but does everything for them. They try to create the path they think their child needs in order to succeed instead of allowing them to figure it out on their own. While that is difficult for a first-time parent, or even an experienced parent, it is necessary for the child's identity and sense of self-worth. Trying to manipulate situations in order to achieve the desired outcome does not help anyone in the long run; it only causes more damage to the child.

Empowering Your Child's Choices

The older your child gets, the more their curiosity begins to wane, and as they age, they learn that there are rules, boundaries, and expectations to be followed. This shapes their lives and the outcome of their futures. While your toddler is still young, able to be influenced positively, and malleable enough to shape themselves the way they want, it is best to empower your child's choices. Empowering them consists of mutual respect, self-discipline, or sufficiency, as well as the freedom to choose the right objective for them based on their emotional state.

Understanding your toddler's needs and wants is key to helping with their success. If they feel that they have you in their corner, then the child is more likely to pick the outcome that is best for them because they feel secure in their parents' support of them. Gentle encouragement toward the child will go a long way. Empowerment helps contribute to the toddler's confidence and demonstrates that they should not second-guess themselves. Their voices, opinions, and wants are important and should never be put second to someone else's.

Many times children forget that they should put themselves first at the appropriate time, and may instead allow others to walk over them or shape their experiences. By empowering your child's choices, you are contributing to a healthy sense of self-worth and understanding that the toddler's wants and needs are important. By doing this, the child becomes more aware of what is best for them instead of feeling confused or lost.

Applauding Both Wins and Losses

Win or lose, both need to be applauded and recognized. When the child makes an error, applaud them. When your child fails a test in school, applaud them. This may sound absurd as we have been told to *only* applaud the wins, but how are children supposed to achieve that success without failure? In order to be grateful for a win, they may first have to accept a loss. By applauding your child's mistakes, you are creating awareness that missteps are okay and teaching them that they have nothing to feel ashamed of. Mistakes are part of growth. Instead of being frightened to make mistakes that cause them to stop trying, encourage the mistake. Encourage them with the "try and try again" mentality.

Depending upon the severity of the error, not all losses should be encouraged—for instance, hurting someone, continuously failing in school, etc.—but they should be accepted as part of growing up. Toddlers will make mistakes. They are young and still developing the awareness that their actions result in consequences. They look to their parents for guidance, acceptance, and understanding. If their parents are always shaming them for failing, they will become stressed and anxious as they age. The toddler will see the praise from the success—passing a test, making new friends, asking for help, etc.—and wonder why they are treated better for that. This creates a distance between the self and the whole, forcing the child to question if their value is only determined by their successes. Please try to avoid that, as no child should feel that way.

The Montessori method helps with this by actually encouraging parents to applaud both instead of just the wins. By treating the child equally in both situations, you are helping to create a balance they desperately need in their lives. Toddlers will learn as they are smart and observant, and they will see which errors are applauded and which ones are not and will learn from each. Experience is everything. Positive or negative, they will learn from it. There is no such thing as a silly idea or stupid plan; if the toddler wants to try it, let them while also demonstrating the possible outcome. If they are aware that there is the possibility of failure but that their parents are okay with it, they are less likely to stress themselves out over the possibility of failure and are more likely to feel confident and safe in taking a risk.

Chapter 5:

Empowerment

Supporting your child's development is key to their success. Development comes with time; it is a slow process that adapts as the child learns. As a parent, you sometimes forget to empower your child and instead focus on how you can keep them safe and guide them. While a toddler needs that in their life as they are not fully capable of doing it themself, they also need to feel empowered to be independent. Empowerment is many things, but the definition according to the Merriam-Webster dictionary is "the process of becoming stronger and more confident, especially in controlling one's life and claiming one's choices." Understand that by giving some authority and autonomy to the child, you are allowing them to feel empowered. They see that as an act of respect, and it helps regulate the child when they need to make an important decision. Within the Montessori method, there are ten strategies used to encourage the child. A few of the fundamentals are

- respect for self, peers, and teachers
- independence and independent problem-solving
- respect for our environments
- freedom within limits

- self-discipline and self-motivation

- respect for knowledge and the process for acquiring it (Jiwani-Ali, 2021)

These fundamentals are key to ensuring that both the child and their peers are safe, happy, and learning in a way that suits them best. Empowerment is a strong tool and a method that is highly recommended in the Montessori discipline because children can be more susceptible to energy when they are young. This means that if their parents, peers, or teachers are upset with or worried about them, the child can sense those feelings. They are aware of energies, and it changes the way they view themselves. Either creating a negative viewpoint towards themselves—for instance, the child may begin to believe they are stupid, unworthy, or that there is something wrong with them—or they may become quiet and reserved because they are processing their feelings. They may even become angry or violent. However, if there is positive energy then the toddler will feel empowered. They will begin to understand that no matter what, they have control in their life.

As previously mentioned, there are ten ways to help empower your child. The six previously listed are the fundamentals and the ones most talked about. However, all ten are important to be aware of:

- **Freedom of choice.** Try to allow your child to decide on things such as their own routines, their own snacks, and what to wear. Instead of telling your child to do something, give them a choice: "Do you want to watch a movie before bed or read a story?" This helps the child feel in control, and they get to decide what they want instead of feeling trapped in a decision they may or may not have wanted.

- **Let your child problem-solve**. Instead of doing something for them or showing them how it is done, let your toddler figure it out on their own. Within the Montessori method this is *highly* recommended as it encourages the child to be aware of real risks and consequences should they make a poor choice.

- **Allow risk-taking**. Children will always be covered in bruises, scrapes, and cuts. That is part of their growing-up experience. It can be hard to see your child hurting; however, if you scold or shame them for taking a risk it may stop the toddler from taking that risk, but it will also cause them to fear you. If the parent laughs it off and mentions that it could have been far worse and that they should be careful, this is allowing the child to see that there are serious repercussions to their actions, but that it is up to them to decide.

- **Build awareness of the environment**. This goes back to the discussion of empowerment. The Montessori method highly recommends this concept because it allows the child to explore and experience every environment they encounter. It also helps them become more aware of their limits and gain respect for the individuals around them. Challenging your toddler in an intellectual manner is key to keeping them entertained and intrigued by their environment. It also helps them to understand boundaries, limits, and reasonable reactions to different situations.

- **Listen to your child for real**. As a parent, you may like to believe that you are listening to your child, but are you really? Do you have deep, engaging conversations with them? Are you always telling them no? Do you ever agree with them? Having healthy conversations with your child helps them strengthen their bonds with their peers, especially in the classroom. The Montessori method believes that children have important things to say and that their voices matter. This helps the child become more thoughtful of what they say and how they relay that message without harming others.

- **Help eliminate stereotypes**. Stereotypes and judgments are usually formed due to preconceived notions from the parents. Children will begin associating these judgments with their peers as early as three years of age. In order to circumvent this, the Montessori method creates an all-ages classroom, which means that regardless of size, age, gender, ethnicity, or family history, they all occupy the same environment and have the same opportunities. This creates an inclusive environment versus an exclusive environment.

- **Encourage perseverance**. "Try and try again." Just as in your adult life, your toddler will get frustrated or feel discouraged if they struggle with a task. This can cause them to feel frustrated and give up. Make sure to empower them to keep trying and not to give up easily as this will help develop a strong work ethic later in life. They will be able to persevere through failure, mistakes, or setbacks and will only use those things as motivation to keep pushing forward.

- **Let them pursue interests**. If your child has something that they are talented at and that they have a passion for, let them do it! Try not to sabotage that dream by calling it unrealistic or making them feel that they are aiming too high. Definitely mention that there could be some difficulties along the way and that success takes time, but encourage them to keep pursuing that dream, even if it feels impossible; because, honestly, it's probably not.

- **Nurture a love for learning**. The Montessori method highly recommends that parents try to foster "a love for learning and instill lifelong respect, appreciation, and desire for knowledge" for their child. This helps the child to connect more to an activity simply through the joy they receive from it. By ensuring they are excited about what they are being taught, you are helping them acquire confidence within themself and what they want out of their life.

- **Be excited for your child**. The highest form of empowerment for your child is to be excited when they are. This shows them that you care, that you are involved in their life, and that their feelings are valid. Many psychologists have come to the realization that empathy begins to develop as young as two years old; this is when the child becomes aware of the effect they have upon their parents and vice versa. By using your authority to empower your child, you can help increase their self-esteem and see that whatever they want in life, they can achieve (Jiwani-Ali, 2021).

Feeling empowered by a person of authority, from a toddler's perspective, is extremely rewarding as they are able to distinguish between responsibility and fun. When a child begins to do an activity for fun instead of for obligatory reasons, then they have begun to transition into intrinsic motivation.

Encouraging Intrinsic Motivation

Intrinsic motivation "refers to doing something because it is inherently interesting or enjoyable" (Ryan & Deci, 2000). Delving deeper into this definition, behaviorists have noted that this type of behavior is mostly found in infants. They are constantly trying to grasp, touch, throw, or bite every new thing they encounter. This is their way of understanding because they cannot yet ask questions about the object. By encouraging the toddler to be more intrinsically motivated, adults are helping them find more fun in certain activities rather than worrying about their fundamental value or external influences.

It helps to differentiate between intrinsic motivation—which is internal—and extrinsic motivation. Intrinsic motivation is doing things for fun, to enjoy the object or situation, or to learn from it. External motivation is the opposite; it is simply to gain a desired outcome. Both are important to a toddler while they develop, but external motivation and influences can become too difficult for their minds to comprehend, which can then cause them stress. The intrinsic portion of motivation begins to fade as they age, which is when the external portion becomes more prominent; adults tend to do things for the desired outcome instead of for fun.

Encouraging your toddler to have fun and explore new scenarios helps them to understand their surroundings, their needs, and their curiosities. It also increases their developmental skills. Children are naturally curious and will always try new things because the world is new and exciting to them. By helping them decipher the external from the internal, parents are able to guide their child and help them decide for themselves what is best.

Still Supporting Your Child to Decide Things Themselves

The concept of supporting your child in deciding things for themselves consists of providing choices, friendships, food, experiences, and more. As a toddler, they are prone to accidents, exploring, and even creating as many new experiences as they can. That is what children do. They live. They experience want to experience things for themselves. Sometimes as a parent that scares you because you want the best possible outcome for your child, you want them to always be safe, and you want them to be happy. You do not want to see them hurt, scared, or confused, but sometimes those uncomfortable feelings lead to learning and growth.

Empowering your child with intrinsic motivation and supporting your toddler both fall into the same category. That support is important to them, they crave it. Allowing your child to have a reasonable and age-appropriate amount of freedom encourages the child to be independent. For example, say that the child has dreams to become an astronaut, actor, writer, or artist. Encourage them to follow that dream. There may be people who question it, who ask them later in life what money there is to get out of it, but that does not matter. If the child feels motivated from a young age to follow their dream and do everything possible to achieve it, then they will not care what others say because they know they have the support of those who matter most: mom and dad.

Allowing your child to feel in control of their choices is another form of empowerment. By giving your toddler the power to decide what is important to them and what activities and choices they want to pursue, you are reinforcing their independence. You do not have to give full control, but try not to restrict them from trying something they want to try as this may cause more problems later on. Some tips for supporting your child to make their own decisions are

- Let your child make their own schedule.

- Ask your child if they would rather brush their teeth before or after storytime.

- Let the toddler make friends and try to diffuse an argument should one arise.

- See if they are able to keep prejudices away when meeting people of different abilities or races. If they are struggling, then kindly step in and redirect them to more appropriate words and behavior.

- Help the child understand what their emotional needs are by allowing them to explore. Curiosity is their biggest strength as a child.

There are several more; however, these are just some of the simpler examples. Parents do not always realize that overstepping their child's boundaries can create a negative response from their toddler. To avoid that, give them the space and freedoms to gain the respect and knowledge needed when it comes to understanding the world around them.

Empowering Your Child's Choices

Empowerment of choice, as has been mentioned previously, is ideal for a toddler who is seeking to understand their environment and experience all new ideas, topics, or relationships. In order to ensure that the child is on the right path, parents need to understand that there is a balance, a fine line between freedom with limits or total control. Empowerment aids in confidence, self-discipline, and empathy. By empowering the child you are showing them how to be aware of their peers and their feelings, how to keep judgments to a minimum, and to understand that not everyone functions the same way. Every child is different, but they deserve to be treated equally. That is why the Montessori method recommends that parents teach their toddlers this from the start. Starting at two years old, encourage your child to be eager to learn, empathetic, and open-minded to the thousands of possibilities before them.

Giving your toddler choice and freedom is essential because it helps

- build the child's confidence for future decision-making

- allow the child to feel satisfaction and pride—the child will feel a greater sense of satisfaction in knowing that they made a choice or decision independently

- allow the child to experience a sense of ownership over the decision, activity, or consequence

- allow for greater opportunities to learn through natural consequences—if the child makes a poor decision, often they will learn or gain experience from the process and outcome

- boost self-image—the child begins to see themself as a capable decision maker

- demonstrate your trust in the child which allows the child to trust themself as they begin to understand they have the ability to make decisions

- provide practical skills in decision-making such as weighing options and considering risks

- promote independence and independent thought—a child who is practiced at making a decision in the presence of an adult is more likely to feel confident to make a decision in the absence of an adult

- demonstrate respect for the child's natural and developmental needs

- empower the child.

- give the child control over their body

- allow the child to become more in tune with their body so they begin to be able to tell how much energy they have, when they are hungry, if they are tired, etc., and act on it

- increase engagement and participation—if the child freely chooses an activity that is relevant and of interest to them, it's likely they will engage more with it than with an activity chosen by the adult

- assist the child in furthering an interest or skill that the adult isn't aware of or hasn't considered or allowed for

- respect the child's ability to make a choice

- encourage strong and respectful relationships— if the child is involved in and surrounded by respectful relationships, they are more likely to establish respectful relationships themselves in the future; respectful relationships can be adult/child but also child/child

- promote creativity—if a child is continuously following instructions, they cease to think for themselves, but if the child is continuously offered a choice, they are more likely to seek out new ideas and different ways of doing things, and they are learning to think for themselves, allowing for more creative thought and greater possibilities

- lead the child to feeling fulfilled and at peace—when the child's developmental needs are met, the child will feel fulfilled and content

- reduce conflict—when a child feels they have been heard and listened to, they are less likely to engage in conflict or react in an aggressive way

- demonstrate that the child is important and valued, as are their thoughts and opinions (*Notes to a Montessori parent—give the child a choice!*, 2018).

Each fundamental aspect of empowerment is key to a toddler growing up in a happy, encouraging environment where they feel secure enough to ask for what they need without fear of being belittled by those in power.

Applauding Both Wins and Losses

For many years, parents have used praise and reward systems with their children. In this kind of system, if the child does a good job, they get some kind of reward like a sticker, a sweet candy, or a toy. Most of these are followed by verbal praise such as "good job" or "I'm proud of you." While this type of system can be effective, it only seems to work for so long. Children are smart; they will figure out the pattern eventually: "If I do this, then I get that!" And before you know it, the reward becomes less and less effective. They may begin to want more or bigger rewards. In the article "Motivate Children Without Praise," Karen Disney states (2019):

> When we motivate with praise and rewards and other types of **external motivators**, *children are not learning more about themselves when they accomplish a new task, they are simply learning what it takes to please adults.* They lose interest over time *because they figure it out*: Do **this** and get **that**. The end. That was easy. On the other hand, a child who learns to listen to his *own* voice develops **internal motivation** and learns to push himself to try harder, celebrate his victories, and acknowledge his shortcomings.

This teaches children that perseverance is the way to go. If they are constantly being rewarded and not learning to enjoy the intrinsic reward of pushing their limits, then they are learning to become lazy and only do things for the expected reward at the end. If they rely on rewards, they can become entitled and begin to push for bigger rewards that stimulate their desire to achieve the task, but eventually, that excitement wears off so they begin to push again for bigger and better rewards. No rewards are better; even though that sounds contradictory, it's the truth. Applauding the wins and losses is important as it sheds light on the child's limits, helps them learn, and provides them with their own moral compass. It engages the child enough to understand their own voice and follow their instincts.

Chapter 6:

Misbehavior

Recognizing that misbehavior is natural and inevitable will help parents effectively raise their young children and helps parents to differentiate between natural and learned behaviors. Misbehavior occurs quite frequently in childhood and does not fade away entirely as they reach adolescence. There will always be mistakes made as children are always going to act out to test their boundaries; that is part of their evolutionary process. Understanding that misbehavior is not necessarily a bad thing is useful for parents because much of the time children misbehave because they do not know any better. They are following examples from their peers and trying to understand what is acceptable and what is not. Toddlers are creatures of habit, and they will do as they please because they are curious and love to try new things; that being said, they are more likely to misbehave out of interest or wanting to fit in than they are out of spite.

Misbehavior can also be viewed as a cry for help. As toddlers, most children are not able to verbalize what they want, need, or are scared of. That stems from them still developing their language skills. This can cause frustration within the child, which leads to fierce outbursts, screaming, crying, hitting, and other undesired behaviors. A toddler cannot yet express these emotions any other way because they simply do not know how. Some basics of toddler misbehavior that are helpful to understand are the following:

- Misbehavior can stem from the child feeling as if the parent is taking them away from something they were enjoying—such as a play date or playing at the park.

- They have not quite mastered the skill of understanding their internal thoughts or feelings, which causes negative reactions.

- When the child is reacting in a manner that causes the parent irritation or frustration, it usually stems from a physical need, i.e. they are tired, hungry, need their diaper changed, etc.

- Try to offer affection when they are emotional; usually, the child is seeking connection and that is the only way they know how to ask for it.

- A healthy relationship with you is the only place the toddler will learn manners and find the confidence to ask for help in better ways.

Prioritizing Misbehaviors

Certain misbehaviors from children are usually a form of biological need. They react to how they are feeling because they cannot express that to their parents just yet. In order to understand their misbehavior, you need to understand what it is they need. That is what we call prioritizing misbehavior. Prioritizing what is needed for the child before correcting their behavior. This helps the toddler feel heard and seen. If you punish them directly then they are more likely to misbehave out of anger and resentment, which becomes a learned behavior.

Accidental or natural versus learned behaviors will be explored more later, but for now, remember that children misbehave because that is their way of communicating, and they also misbehave because they do not know any better. So instead of rushing to conclusions and aiming to punish them for what appears to be misbehavior, try to understand why they did what they did and whether it was intentional or simply a plea for attention.

Deciding What Behaviors Are Accidental or Natural and What Is Learned Behavior

Behavior is both learned and natural, which begins the debate of nature versus nurture, but that is a whole different topic. As a toddler, it is safe to say that most of their outbursts are natural; they simply do not have the tools to express themselves otherwise or to manage big emotions right away. However, there are instances where their reaction to an experience is learned behavior. For example, you might take your toddler to the grocery store and they see candy or a toy they want and ask for it. Your first response is usually no because it is too expensive or unnecessary. The toddler will then begin to ask again or point to it, and if they continuously get the "no" response, they may begin to cry or throw a tantrum.

Now, the tantrum is not a learned behavior; it is natural. Toddlers throw fits because they are frustrated, but if the parent gives in to their child's actions by granting them what they wanted just because they want the tantrum to stop, then the tantrum becomes a learned behavior because the child has learned it is a way to get what they want. Sometimes giving them what they want may seem easier than saying no and having everyone look at you because your child is screaming, but you are actually doing a disservice to your toddler by giving in. Instead, when they begin to cry, try to find something to distract them with. Find some way to keep their minds preoccupied before their emotions become too much. You can play I Spy, have a coloring book on you, ask them about their day, or even come prepared with a snack or small toy just in case a situation like this occurs. This keeps them focused and stimulated so that they do not become overwhelmed by the desire to have everything they see.

One tantrum can be considered natural, but if they continue, then it becomes learned behavior because they know that they will get what they want. Differentiating between learned or natural behaviors can be tricky. A few terms to be aware of when understanding behavior are

- exploration
- orientation
- order
- imagination
- manipulation of objects
- repetition
- precision
- control of error leading to perfection
- communication (*Understanding your child's misbehavior as a plea for connection*, 2021)

These are basic instincts in all children. Understanding these can help a parent to understand why their child reacts the way they do towards certain situations and find the right method to help them stop the cycle.

Not Enforcing Harsh Punishments

After understanding why your toddler behaves the way they do, the next step is to figure out how to explain to them why that behavior is unacceptable. The term punishment comes into play here. Many parents use punishment as a negative reinforcement to "straighten out" their child, but really all it does is create bigger issues later on. For example, perhaps the toddler had a tantrum in the grocery store (like the one in the previous example); instead of yelling at the child or telling them that they can never come back to the store with mommy again or that they will get their toys taken away, wait until you have come home and the child has calmed down, and then use a gentle but firm voice to explain why that behavior was not okay. Explain that screaming for what they want is not acceptable, and if someone says no then they must accept that. Try to remove the element of embarrassment for the child as that embarrassment tends to increase their screaming or resistant behavior.

If the toddler is still unable to understand, then try a different method, one that their brains can comprehend. There is no need for harsh punishments; the stern talking-to is enough for most toddlers as seeing their parents disappointed with them makes them upset. Try to resolve the problem without creating a bigger scene or engaging in a power struggle with your toddler. They do not know any better. They are simply seeking attention and have yet to figure out that there is a better way to ask for it. Punishment and behavior go together—if the child knows that there is a severe punishment, chances are they will not do it again; however, this can create anger within the child, and they may begin to resist or test the limits of that punishment.

If the punishment is light but still holds serious value, then they will understand that what they did was not okay, that there are consequences to their actions, but that they do not have to feel bad about themself because of it. This was a learning experience. That inner voice will later remind them not to do it, which will hopefully remind the child that poor behavior is not acceptable.

Chapter 7:

Life, Simulated

As we wrap up these lessons, it's important to realize that reflecting on our lives is not something many people do regularly, but it is the first step to ensuring the child is prepared for their future. Internalizing your own behavior and reactions toward your child can be difficult. Most people understand that raising a child is no easy task. To all parents out there, you guys deserve medals! It can be difficult to recognize your successes as a parent because you feel as if there is more to be done or that perhaps you have made certain mistakes you wish you hadn't. You are human, and you are bound to make mistakes. Understanding and implementing the seven elements of the Montessori method of discipline is the beginning of helping yourself as well as your child. To refresh the seven steps are

- environment
- communication
- responsibility
- freedom
- empowerment

- misbehavior

- life, simulated

Environment refers to their surroundings and what sort of experiences they will or may face during their life and how it can be deliberately created in order to help that toddler build life skills. Communication seems self-explanatory: Talk about what is wrong with your toddler in a manner in which they are able to process and understand. Your toddler speaks with you too, just not always with words. Their body language is their communication until they are old enough to form words. Responsibility: both you and your child have a responsibility. Your child is responsible for themself, for their actions, behaviors, and wants. You, the adult, are responsible for the same things for yourself as well as for modeling these things for your child. Your reaction to your child dictates their behavior later on, which we now know is called learned behavior (or nurture).

Freedom is a really important element of the Montessori method. Toddlers need to have freedom to understand who they are as a person and what they wish to gain from their life within reason. If they are trapped by harsh rules and unforgiving boundaries, then they are more likely to lash out. Empowerment goes with freedom. Encourage your toddler to pursue what they want in life as long as it doesn't hurt themself or others. Show them that you are supportive and not judgmental. Misbehavior is a learning process for both the adult and the child. Natural behaviors change over time as children age they mature, but learned behaviors?

Those are harder to break. And finally, life, simulated is simply understanding where your child is currently in their development and making sure they are ready for what is about to come next.

Ensuring Your Child Is Ready for Real Life

No parent ever feels like their child is ready to take on the heaviness of life. There is always going to be concern or worry, something to pick on or critique. But there comes a point in your child's life where you have to let them go. They will learn that things are not always as they seem and that if they work hard, are good people, and try to be grateful for what they have, life will be pretty decent. Children need to learn that sometimes expecting things from others will lead to disappointment. People may let them down, but if the child holds no expectations for how others should act, then they will be happier. Children must learn to only create expectations for themselves and that theirs is the only opinion that matters. Helping your child get the necessary tools they need, fostering a love for learning, and providing the space for them to test their boundaries is the path to success.

Many believe that education and a well-paying job are the way to achieve happiness or success, but that isn't always the case. Being okay with who you are is what matters. As a parent, it is your job to teach your child to love themself and others for who they are without harsh judgments or expectations. This will help your toddler to center themself when life begins to become too overwhelming. It is not easy to try and prepare someone for life; there may not be a "ready to take on the world" approach, but what you can do for your child is make sure that they understand the difficulties that lie ahead and that not everything will be easy to understand. Let them know that making mistakes is normal and that no matter what, you will always be there to support them.

Ensuring These Lessons Will Mean They Can Think for Themselves

Learning to think for yourself and having someone tell you what to think are two completely different things. Toddlers may expect mom and dad to do things for them as they are not yet able to. However, they do have a mind of their own, and they are able to begin questioning what it is they have experienced. By teaching your toddler to become more self-sufficient, you are encouraging your toddler to create personal thought and trust in their own intelligence because they begin to see that they can rely on themself. If they grow up depending on others to do everything for them, then the child will grow up spoiled, entitled, and incapable of functioning by themselves. This is a bad thing, and life will not take it easy on them.

Some lessons and qualities that can be passed on to your child are respect, patience, perseverance, hard work, open-mindedness, empathy, and strength. These characteristics create the type of person who is able to stand up for themselves, who knows what they want, and who is open to learning about other people and cultures. Creating the proper methods to ensure that your child is capable of doing things without adult intervention and that they are ready to face the world is the goal of every parent. Life is not meant to be easy, simple, or just handed to you on a silver plate; there are going to be pitfalls, failures, setbacks, and losses, but it is what you do with those experiences that make you ready for life. As a toddler, it may seem impossible; the world is so large and vast and imposing that it can become overwhelming or scary. But they soon learn that they can do anything. They have that freedom and that empowerment from you, the parent, to test their limits and to figure out what it is they are meant to do with their lives.

Those types of lessons are important. They help to ensure that the child will grow up with the abilities to think logically and realistically while also not being afraid to try the "unrealistic" aspects. Sometimes children lose their creativity, they lose that magic; encourage them to keep it because it is that sort of openness that will benefit them in the end. Obviously, everything has limits, but try not to rob your toddler of their dreams. Encourage it while also making sure they have a "Plan B" that they are just as enthusiastic about.

Allowing Them to Be Able to Be Free in Life to Do Things

As Maria Montessori said:

> Let the children be free; encourage them; let them run outside when it is raining; let them remove their shoes when they find a puddle of water; and when the grass of the meadows is wet with dew, let them run on it and trample it with their bare feet; let them rest peacefully when a tree invites them to sleep beneath its shade; let them shout and laugh when the sun wakes them in the morning.

This is what Montessori meant when she stated that children should be free to do things in life. They are children, they are curious, they are young and beautiful. Why restrict them from experiencing the small joys in life because of the social propriety of it? Children are meant to be children. They are not meant to be anything else. Giving them the freedom to explore and discover what life has to offer is one of the key aspects of the Montessori method. Freedom and empowerment: These two work together well as one gives the child the range to explore and understand the world around them, while the other gives them the courage and strength to keep going and to trust their voice of reason and not doubt themselves.

Freedom is a beautiful tool. Not many parents allow full freedom as they are worried about their toddlers—and rightfully so, as they are still young—but restricting your toddler is the same as restricting a teenager. There will be anger, resentment, distance, and problems later on. The one major difference is that a teenager can communicate their anger, and that is when things get really ugly—but that is a topic for another book. People are sometimes not able to see themselves clearly until they examine themselves through the eyes of others. Toddlers are the same way. Unless you point out what went wrong, they will keep doing it. Show your child that they have you and will always have you and that they are the ones in control of their own decisions. This helps them feel ready for what will come later in life, even if it is just for the experience of tomorrow. Every day counts. Every new challenge matters. Try not to let them navigate it alone or make them feel like they are missing out because there are too many rules; that sense of "I'm missing out" is just as detrimental for the child as any other punishment or setback.

Conclusion

The Montessori method is highly recommended by child psychologists all over the world as it is a clean, precise method on how to raise a smart, curious, and responsible child. As this book has stated, there are seven steps to the Montessori method, each one with a subcategory to explain the idea further. To reiterate some of the key takeaways, let's go over the seven aspects of the Montessori method once again:

- **Misbehavior.** This is when a parent has to decide if their child's response is learned or natural. They also have to learn to not use bribes or harsh punishments that may only cause them to react worse. You want to build *intrinsic* (internal) motivation instead of *extrinsic* (external) motivation.

- **Respectful communication.** Talk to your child the way you would like them to speak to you. If you shout to resolve a problem, chances are they will shout when faced with a problem. Instead, let them know that you see and value them and that they can rely on you to keep them safe. This establishes respect in the parent-child relationship as you both have learned how to understand one another.

- **Model/assist the child to make amends.** This is when the child watches what their parents do and copies it. For example, if someone is crying, you try to comfort them. Eventually, the child will learn to do this on their own as if it were second nature, and the parents are around to assist should the child need it.

- **Find ways to solve problems together.** Instead of using bribery (an overused strategy that only works temporarily), why not use something more productive like asking your child to help with a task or other things that can keep the child engaged and feeling part of the activity or task. The satisfaction of seeing your parents happy and self-praise should work as most children want to see their parents happy and want to feel like they did a good job.

- **Help your child if they are finding things too difficult.** This can range anywhere from solving a homework question to soothing them after a big tantrum. Either way, make sure you are there to help your child in whatever way they need it.

- **Freedom with limits.** This is important. Allowing your child to have the freedom to explore, touch, and experience their surroundings is key to them understanding their world. To get the desired results, there needs to be freedom, which may mean making sure the child and others around them are safe without entrapping the child within so many rules.

- **Translate for them.** Behavior is a form of communication, and in order for the toddler to understand someone else's body language, the parent needs to step in to help. For example, if another toddler is playing with a toy and your child wants it, tell them that the toy is unavailable right now but they can have a turn later. This helps stop fights and screaming as the toddler will understand that it's not that they cannot play with the toy, they just cannot use it right now.

- **Kind and clear limits.** Set limits with your child to ensure good behavior and curb bad habits. If the child wants to scream, find a form of communication that lets them know that screaming is not an acceptable way to handle emotions and suggest an alternative way that is acceptable to release that frustration. Label for them what behaviors and responses are acceptable and what are not; be consistent to create stability and predictability for your toddler. Label the limits of what is acceptable and what is not to help create stability for your toddler.

Everyone will interpret these lessons differently, and that is okay; use them within your daily parenting life how you see fit. Each chapter delved into one of the aspects of Montessori discipline, and within each chapter there were subsections that expanded on each aspect. Trying to determine how to raise your child the best that you can within your abilities without limiting them is not easy. Many parents struggle with this, and that is okay! Empowerment, remember? Try and try again. Just because you slipped up once does not mean you have permanently damaged your child. No, it just means that there is a learning curve and a process to follow. Everyone is different, and each child is different. No two are exactly the same. If you are hesitant and worried, then your child will be too. They are highly susceptible to your emotions and most of their world revolves around your opinions of them.

Understand this: no one is perfect. It is okay to make an error, do not be so critical of yourself if you feel that you let your child down. You did not. Children are resilient. However, if you continue to make the mistakes you know are not the most beneficial to your child's development, then that is where trust begins to break down. If you are telling your child to have healthy reactions to certain situations, and yet here you are yelling at them over their every mistake, it becomes confusing for the child and they will begin to behave in the way that is modeled for them rather than the way you are telling them to behave. This is where the problems start. The Montessori discipline has been set in place so that new parents, and experienced ones, can find better ways to help their children and to ensure that their child is prepared for life by providing the tools needed to allow them to understand their own physical, emotional, and social needs.

Parents, having kids is not easy. Raising them is not easy. But what you can do is find the right tools to help them and guide them and allow them to have the freedom to create their own paths. Empowerment (one of the most-used words in this book) is something that seems to be pushed to the side too often. Try to help your child more instead of pushing them away. Some examples of this might look like the following:

- Encourage the child to push beyond what they believe to be their own physical limitations. What they think is the end of their abilities is usually not. Create an environment that is set up for the child so that they feel in control and have the freedom to choose what they want.

- Instead of saying "Good job" and clapping your hands as praise for their good decision or achievement (this is considered an extrinsic reward and later becomes ineffective for the child), try to empower them so that they feel like they did this for themselves and not for external gain. If they feel that a reward is necessary, the child may become lazy and not try to achieve their greatest potential.

- Communication is key. Your toddler is always communicating with you, you just have to learn to understand their language. Communication creates identity and a sense of self-awareness for the child. This is helpful when they begin their journeys in a social environment.

Discipline is needed throughout our entire lives, not just in childhood. These methods can be used with teenagers and even adults, perhaps with some modifications, but the principles will still be the same. Everyone will understand the lessons differently; some may stick strictly to the rules, others may be more lenient, but both are fine. It does not matter how you choose to implement these lessons as long as you use them. Montessori toddler discipline has helped many parents and children. It is used in classrooms and even entire schools and is viewed as the method to use when children are involved. Understanding the basic physical and psychological needs of your child is the biggest step to helping them succeed and be ready for what life has in store for them.

References

Chipwood, D. (2018, June 5). *A Montessori approach to discipline.* Living Montessori Now. https://livingmontessorinow.com/a-montessori-approach-to-discipline/

Craycroft, M. (n.d.). *How to discipline effectively in a Montessori environment.* Carrots Are Orange. https://carrotsareorange.com/montessori-discipline/

Disney, K. (2019, August 6). *Motivate children without praise and rewards.* Children's House Montessori School of Reston. https://childrenshouse-montessori.com/2019/08/06/motivate-children-without-praise-and-rewards/

Empowerment. (n.d.) Merriam-Webster. https://www.merriam-webster.com/dictionary/empowerment.

Historical Snapshots. (2018, August 31). *Maria Montessori: "Let the children be free."* Historical Snapshots. https://historicalsnaps.com/2018/08/31/maria-montessori-let-the-children-be-free/

Human needs and tendencies. (2021). Age of Montessori. https://ageofmontessori.org/human-needs-and-tendencies/

Jiwani-Ali, S. (2021, November 10). *10 ways to make your child feel empowered.* Mosaic Montessori Academy. https://mosaicmontessori.ca/10-ways-to-make-your-child-feel-empowered/

Karchmar Cameron, L. (2017, June 22). *7 fundamentals of a Montessori lesson.* Montessori Rocks. https://montessorirocks.org/7-fundamentals-of-a-montessori-lesson/

A Montessori approach to discipline. (2022). The Montessori Notebook. https://www.themontessorinotebook.com/montessori-approach-to-discipline/

Notes to a Montessori parent—give the child a choice! (2018, May 18). How We Montessori; Parenting. https://www.howwemontessori.com/how-we-montessori/2018/05/montessori-give-the-child-a-choice.html

Ryan, R. M. & Deci, E. L. (2000). *Intrinsic and extrinsic motivations: Classic definitions and new directions.* Science Direct. https://doi.org/10.1006/ceps.1999.1020

The ten secrets of Montessori—#6 the prepared environment. (2021). Age of Montessori. https://ageofmontessori.org/the-ten-secrets-of-montessori-6-the-prepared-environment/

The ten secrets of Montessori—#8 liberty and discipline. (2021). Age of Montessori. https://ageofmontessori.org/liberty-discipline/

Understanding your child's misbehavior as a plea for connection. (2021). Age of Montessori. https://ageofmontessori.org/understanding-childs-misbehavior-plea-connection/

Made in the USA
Monee, IL
11 September 2023